MW00913925

Blues/Rock
Improv

taught by...

Jon Finn

CD contents

[1]	Tune-Up	[10]	Turnaround #6
[2]	Rhythm Part 1	[11]	Turnaround #7
[3]	Rhythm Part 2	[12]	Turnaround #8
[4]	Rhythm Part 3	[13]	Soloing Exercise #1
[5]	Turnaround #1	[14]	Soloing Exercise #2
[6]	Turnaround #2	[15]	Soloing Exercise #3
[7]	Turnaround #3	[16]	The Solo
[8]	Turnaround #4	[17]	Backing Tracks (no solo)
[9]	Turnaround #5		

The Players on the CD
Jeff MacPherson - Drums
Paul Pasmore - Bass
Jon Finn - Guitar

1 2 3 4 5 6 7 8 9 0

© 2004 BY MEL BAY PUBLICATIONS, INC., PACIFIC, MO 63069.
ALL RIGHTS RESERVED. INTERNATIONAL COPYRIGHT SECURED. B.M.I. MADE AND PRINTED IN U.S.A.
No part of this publication may be reproduced in whole or in part, or stored in a retrieval system, or transmitted in any form
or by any means, electronic, mechanical, photocopy, recording, or otherwise, without written permission of the publisher.

Visit us on the Web at www.melbay.com — E-mail us at email@melbay.com

BLUES/ROCK IMPROVISATION
jon finn

introduction

Sometimes the best way to learn how to do something is to simply do it. This book will teach you some basics about Blues/Rock soloing. You will learn some basic rhythm guitar parts, the Standard Blues Progression, Turnarounds, some soloing exercises, and a fully transcribed solo. The song included is designed to highlight what I feel are important skills.

Playing Blues/Rock guitar is simple in the same way baseball is simple. In baseball, someone throws a ball while someone else tries to bat it to a place where no-one is standing, then run as far as possible without being caught. The idea itself is very simple but difficult to do well.

So it is with Blues/Rock. Often, a good Blues/Rock solo is little more than a few simple pentatonic rock licks played over a few simple chords. Most guitarists figure that idea out early in their development. Many (myself included for a long time...) make the fatal mistake of thinking that it's "too simple" and not worth our time. Upon closer listening, I've noticed that many Blues/Rock solos have common tendencies (which is the very reason I've written this book). While physically easy to play, the challenge is to come up with your own ideas, follow the tendencies of the style, execute it accurately, and convey the emotion needed to make your performance worth your listener's undivided attention. Herein lies the essential lesson: Simple and easy are not the same.

how to use this book

I've learned some of the most important musical lessons while jamming with friends, hearing them do something really cool and asking, "hey what was that?" I tried to include as many of those here and present them with that spirit in mind.

If you notice that many Blues/Rock tunes follow the same chord progression (often with only minor variations such as different keys, different feels etc.), then you may wonder why this is so. I suspect that a big reason is that in this style, it is unnecessary to "re-invent the wheel." If you look at the mechanics of how the progression works, it becomes clearer why so many songs use it. It just works.

One fundamental element of this style is a vocabulary of turnaround licks. List almost every great Blues/Rock guitarist and you will notice that they very rarely miss an opportunity to play a cool turnaround lick. To do otherwise is a bit like putting a dragster on the Daytona 500 track. You might go really fast but you will lose control pretty quickly!

The next part of the book gives some ideas and strategies to try. Following each idea will get a certain type of sound. The idea is to increase your musical vocabulary through concepts rather than licks. The larger your musical vocabulary is, the more eloquently you can convey your ideas. You will find that doing variations on ideas you already know often produces far more fertile creative flow than simply trying to think of new licks.

Musical concepts make a lot more sense to me if I see an application. By learning the solo, you can draw from it ideas that you can use in your own music in your own way. Playing other people's solos is a great way to get out of your own head for a fresh perspective. Allowing yourself to be inspired by the ideas of others helps keep your mind open. Doing that is always good for your music.

Learn everything contained in this book. Then apply it to your own music in your own way.

Table of Contents

terms to know

This book is written so that information about the techniques are indicated along with the musical transcription. This way, you can see what was done, and why. This makes the notation look a little more crowded than normal. The advantage is that anything you might want to know is likely right in front of you. It is not necessary to understand every last detail in order to move to the next page. Learn what you can, in the way that makes the most sense, and temporarily disregard any information that seems to overwhelm you. For example, if you can only read tab, then work with that until you are ready to look in to the other elements. When you do, each layer of understanding will unfold at a pace ideal to your learning style. All roads really do lead to Rome!

(~ 00:03) - This is a "time stamp." It shows where this music appears on the CD. Use it to match the notation with the CD.

G7, C7, D7 (etc.) - Chord Symbols: Here, you rarely play exact chord fingerings. Rather, the chords are implied by the sum total of both of the rhythm parts played together. The symbols summarize the chord activity and help with understanding and keeping track of song form.

III, IV, V (etc.) - These are called position markers. Indicated between the standard notation and tablature, it is used as a guide for where to place your fret-hand. if "V" is indicated, place your fret hand so your 1st finger is at the 5th fret. This meant to be a guide rather than an absolute reference.

H.O. - Hammer-on: Pick (or pluck) the first note, then "hammer" the fret-hand to sound the next note.

P.O. - Pull-off: Pick (or pluck) the first note, then "pull" the fret-hand finger to sound the next note.

sl. - Slide: Play the first note, then slide the same finger to the next note without picking or plucking.

B - Bend: Fingering one pitch then bending to another. In notation, the fingered note is indicated as a grace note with an arrow pointing toward the target pitch. In the tablature the target note is indicated in parenthesis after the fingered note. The tab also uses arrows to indicate bends. This technique is used quite a lot.

R - Release: The opposite of Bend. Releasing the "bend pressure" to restore the string to it's original pitch. Notated in much the same way as Bend.

⊓ - Down stroke with the pick

V - Up stroke with the pick

1 = 1st fret-hand finger

2 = 2nd (middle) fret-hand finger

3 = 3rd fret-hand finger

4 = 4th (pinky) fret-hand finger

Turnaround - Refers to a musical phrase that "punctuates" the music. One of the primary lessons in this book attempts to teach is how to include that technique in your musical vocabulary.

rhythm guitar part # 1

This is the part that creates the feel of the piece. Everything else that happens around it (bass, drums, other rhythm guitar parts) rely on this as the backbone. By learning the rhythm part, you learn the essence of the tune. You are more aware of your musical surroundings in doing so. Usually a better solo is the result. Here is an analogy: Most people like it when you remember their name. Usually, most don't make it a requirement for them to be friendly to you. If you remember their name, it is like telling them you think they are important to you. That means liking you helps them feel important. How this applies to soloing: Knowing the rhythm parts is like telling the song you think it's important. If you think I am crazy, try it anyway and see what you think!

Note the mechanics of the rhythm lick:

⇨   It is a two-measure rhythmic phrase. In the first measure the accent is on beat "one." Going in to the second measure the "and" of beat "four" is accented to sound like an "anticipation" in to the second measure. It is an effect often used to create rhythmic momentum.

⇨   A "power chord" is played twice in the phrase: once for each rhythmic accent. Knowing this will be meaningful later. A "power chord" is like an harmonic abbreviation often used in rock harmony. Many times guitarists will play power chords interchangeably as major, minor, 7th, minor 7th. In fact it's common for the guitarist to not make any distinction between them if it doesn't affect what they actually play. By playing a power chord at the beginning of each phrase, we are playing the "root" and "fifth" of the chord (A true dominant 7th chord has root, 3rd, 5th, and ♭7).

▸▸ **rhythm guitar part # 1** / CD Track # 2

This part continues through the entire piece.

rhythm guitar part # 2

This part begins at (~00:22) after the first full chorus. It is a very simple part to play. All the notes are played with your 1st and 2nd fingers. All the notes are on the 4th (D) and 3rd (G) strings. When Rhythm Guitar Part # 1 moves to the next chord, this part simply moves one fret up or down through almost all of it (except moving from D7 to C7, and going to the turnaround).

⇨   This phrase, when played alongside the power chords in Rhythm Guitar Part # 1, gives all of the chord tones. On each chord, this part always plays the "7th" and "3rd" of the chord. The interval played in this part is called a "tritone." Moving it in half-steps the function of each note reverses. On the G7, the note played on the 4th string (F) is the "7th" of the chord, and the 3rd string (B) is the "3rd." On the C7, and D7, the 4th string plays the "3rd" (E or F♯ depending on chord) and the 3rd string plays the "7th" (B♭ or C depending on chord). This means that although the part itself is only moving in half-steps, the actual function of the notes are trading places between the power chords in Part #1 playing "root" and "5th", while Part # 2 plays "3rd" and "7th." The combination of the two parts plays the entire chord. Dividing the chord tones between two parts produces a different texture than simply playing the whole chord.

⇨   Since it is a one-measure pattern and "Part # 1" is a two-measure pattern, this creates some rhythmic tension between the two parts. It's a very simple, but effective tool.

rhythm guitar part # 2 / CD Track # 3

Moves in half-steps and highlights chord tones.

rhythm guitar part # 3

This part begins at (~01:19) on tracks 16 and 17. This part is a little more intricate than Rhythm Guitar Part # 2, but functions in much the same way. Like Part # 2, it's purpose is to be a "rhythmic foil" to Part # 1, and to also play the actual chord tones (more specific than simply a power chord).

⇨　　Rhythm Guitar Part #3 is a two-measure phrase that has sort of a "question/answer" feel to it. The first measure uses almost the same phrase as Part # 2. Part # 3 plays more notes and has a slightly looser feel (hammer-ons, etc).

⇨　　This part sets up a little chord progression within a chord progression, called a "cadence." A cadence (loosely defined) is a group of chords that, when played in sequence, set up a "point of rest" by developing a small amount of harmonic tension, then releasing it. I like to think of it this way: If my guitar strings aren't wound tightly enough, they won't vibrate. If they are wound too tight, they will break. The right amount of tension is somewhere in the middle. Also, a small amount of tension is needed in order to create music!

▶▶ **rhythm guitar part # 3** / CD Track # 4

Chord tones with two-bar rhythm pattern.

the standard blues progression

Most guitarists who have played for a few years become at least a little aware of how the Standard 12-bar Blues Progression works. Sometimes though, when we've been looking at something too long, we overlook things that might otherwise seem obvious. Just as it is unnecessary to re-invent the wheel, the 12-bar blues progression is used as often as it is because it works so well.

One often overlooked element of the 12-bar Blues progression is that it builds momentum in much the same way that a wave builds momentum, then finally when the wave crests, the water crashes and the process begins again. The 12-bar Blues progression creates roughly the same effect with the chords.

This page shows the mechanics of a Standard Blues Progression. Conceptually, this is what drives the example given in the book. Here, all of the licks are removed and we look at it from the point of view of chord movement. By doing that, we can see clearly that as we get further in to the progression, the chords get more and more active. Finally the turnaround plays a different chord every beat. You might think when looking at the turnaround, "I can't play that many chords that fast!"

Most players in this style don't play the chords per se. Most of the time, the lead guitarist plays one lick, the bass plays another, the rhythm guitarist plays yet another. The effect of all of those licks played together are the chords (or ones like them) given here.

▸▸ the standard blues progression

Note: "One" (I) chord is held for four measures. This establishes a tonal "home base."

Here, the chords change every two measures; twice as often as the first four measures.

Here, the chords change every measure; again twice as often as the previous four measures.

The turnaround is the climax where chords are changing every beat.

turnarounds

Turnarounds are very deceptive little critters. They are usually easy to understand, and easy to play. Further, when they are played, most people recognize the sound even if they don't know the correct musical term. Almost every guitarist who has tried to play blues knows at least one turnaround.

I once took a lesson from a very well known blues guitarist. One of the things he showed me was "the T-Bone King Turnaround", the "Jimmie James Collins Turnaround" and the "Blind Cantaloupe Smith Turnaround." Of course the examples are fictitious but this teacher was making the point that you have to learn the licks played by those who created the style. At the time I thought a lot about how creatively restricting that can be. I rejected his ideas and moved on. But every time I played blues I felt like there were something missing in my playing. I started noticing that my turnarounds tended to fall in to one of these categories:

1. One of the two I remember learning as a teenager.
2. Partially played but almost missed, sounding like I am just a little behind everyone else.
3. Missing it entirely.

When I started teaching rock guitar at the college level, I rarely talked about blues, because I thought it was too simple to talk about at a college. I didn't want to insult my students. Most of the students I work with are very hard working and usually very talented. Not long ago, I started working on it with some of them; particularly the ones who showed promise as performers. Each of them were very accomplished rock players. They played great solos. Very often their turnarounds fell in to these categories:

1. One of the two they remember learning as a teenager.
2. Partially played but almost missed, sounding like they are just a little behind.
3. Missing it entirely.

This told me a few things about turnarounds. Even though playing the "Blind Cantaloupe Smith Turnaround" may not be the most creative act, doing so does acknowledge the style. Every style of music has it's own musical value system. In Blues, turnaround licks are part of the vocabulary. We can learn to speak Japanese but until we learn the right way to pronounce and phrase the words, it will be obvious we are not from Japan.

Playing a blues turnaround is a bit like musical punctuation. The point is to stop improvising, then play the lick as if to say, "I am now finished with this idea and I am about to move on." Doing that well requires these things of you:

⇨   A readily available vocabulary of blues licks at your disposal.
⇨   Enough focus to see when and where to play it.

The next eight examples show all the turnarounds that have been used for this project. I think it would be a great idea to learn them all, then make up a few of your own.

The list of turnarounds found here are the ones used in the song, both in the rhythm parts and in the solo. They are also used in the Soloing Exercises. Learning them all will give you a good head start in developing your vocabulary of blues turnarounds.

turnarounds

▸ **turnaround # 1** / CD Track # 5

▸ **turnaround # 2** / CD Track # 6

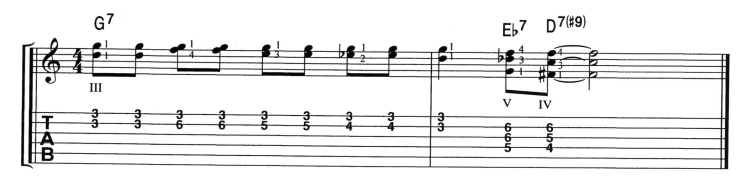

▸ **turnaround # 3** / CD Track # 7

▸ **turnaround # 4** / CD Track # 8

turnarounds cont.

▶▶ **turnaround # 5** / CD Track # 9

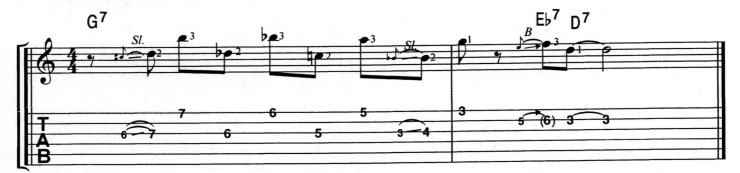

▶▶ **turnaround # 6** / CD Track # 10

▶▶ **turnaround # 7** / CD Track # 11

▶▶ **turnaround # 8** / CD Track # 12

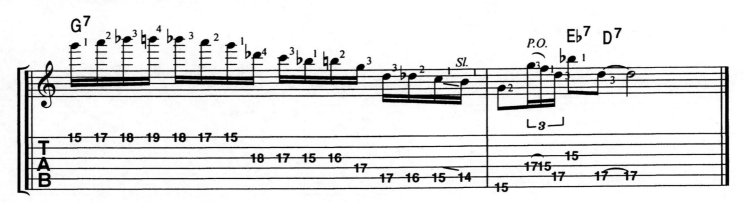

soloing exercises, scales and ideas

This section of the book is meant to give you some ideas to think about when soloing in this style. The way we think always influences what we play. I often hear it said that it's best to "not think" when playing. I agree to a point. But if our minds are wandering off to visions of some tropical island, and we're always getting lost in the song, the audience is bored, and the venue is unimpressed, perhaps we've gone too far!

Each of these exercises is meant to focus on and reinforce skills I think are important. Just as a football player runs through a field of tires to improve his "running and dodging" skills, these are meant to accomplish roughly the same end. As you play these exercises, try to make them as musical sounding as possible. Try to remember their purpose. Doing that might make your playing sound a little less free and creative, and at it's worst, downright stiff. But then try to remember that they rarely play football games with tires in the field!

It is also important to remember that success with these skills may not make you a great player. It depends where you take it. In Martial Arts, there is an expression, "Some train to train, others train to fight."

There is no right way to solo. The right solo is the one where you say to yourself, "Yeah, that was it" after you're finished. I've played hundreds of thousands of solos. Some have said they like what I've done. I have about two that make me think, "That was it." It is a process more than a goal for me.

soloing exercise # 1

Exercise #1: Play anything you want, then stop and play the turnaround.

This sounds much easier than it is. Here we are given permission to do anything provided we play the turnaround in the right spot. In the beginning, focus mostly on playing exactly the turnaround given here. I've noticed that when I think this way, I sound different. If I've decided in advance what turnaround to play, I can "see it coming" while I am playing. This "forces" me to wrap up any phrase I might be playing in order to get to the turnaround.

The turnaround lick itself is not the important part of this lesson. Rather, it is the ability to play it reliably in the middle of your solo each time it comes up.

Usually when I drive my car, it is to accomplish something. If I am out of dish soap, I get in the car and drive to the store and buy some. Driving to the store, I've already decided the route I will take. If a detour comes up it's not a big deal. It just means my original plan won't work because of unforeseen circumstance. When I drive my car for leisure with no destination in mind, it is likely I will end up in an unexpected place (which can be good or bad), or maybe I might end up simply going in circles.

I am not saying that planning your solos is always better. It is simply different.

▶▶ soloing exercise #1 / CD Track # 13

soloing exercise # 2

Exercise #2: Play the minor pentatonic scale that matches the chord, changing positions. Play a different turnaround each time.

Here, you play the same lick over and over, while moving it's position in order to match the chord. It will soon be obvious that you can start varying the licks over each chord while moving. It's a good idea to resist doing so until you are very comfortable playing it as is.

Also, instead of simply playing the same turnaround each time, you start varying the turnarounds. At first I would recommend planning out in advance which turnaround you will play until you can do it without thinking. Next, start choosing the turnaround during each chorus. Start with the turnarounds listed in this book, then make up your own.

➤➤ **soloing exercise #2** / CD Track # 14

soloing exercise # 3

Exercise # 3: Changing the notes in the lick to match the chord without changing positions. Play a different turnaround each time.

As you do this exercise, it may start to sound a little repetitive. You are right. It is. Its purpose is to illustrate how the chord tones can influence the melody. If you remember, Rhythm Guitar Part #2 (Page 9) exploits a half-step movement on the 3rd and 4th strings. Moving those notes in half steps gave us a smooth way to move from G7 to C7 and D7. Knowing that little trick (if you haven't looked at it yet, now might be a great time...) offers some very cool possibilities in soloing. You give the impression that you know exactly where you are. This exercise takes Rhythm Guitar Part # 2 and turns it into a melody.

As with the other exercises, try to plug in different turnarounds. Continue to make up your own and insert them.

When we're practicing, it's important to know what you're trying to accomplish. Sometimes we play to have fun. Other times, we're trying to improve certain skills. When working to improve certain skills, it might be wise to understand that what comes out may not sound ideal at first. I find it does help to remember why I am working on something, and to be patient and diligent with it. Anything worth our time tends to take time to develop.

I also think it's important to maintain a certain amount of fun in your practice session. It helps foster your enthusiasm for music. If its not fun for you, why would anyone else want to listen?

▸▸ **soloing exercise #3** / CD Track # 15

Exercise # 3: Changing the notes in the lick to match the chord without
changing positions. Play a different turnaround each time.

the solo

So many interviews with famous guitarists tend to focus on the idea of not thinking too much. In many ways I agree with the principle. If our sense of reason and logic gets too much in the way our solos can start to sound too planned. Too little spontaneity and that free-wheeling sense of adventure can get lost.

We can also go too far the other way. Following our creative muse with little or no thought to what we are doing can lead to playing that sounds, well, directionless. It's a bit like riding in a car with no destination in mind. We can enjoy the ride, but we shouldn't be surprised if we get lost too.

The approach used here is somewhere in the middle between those two extremes. I recorded the solo first, then transcribed it. While playing it, I did try to keep in the back of my mind this piece is meant to teach some basic Blues/Rock guitar vocabulary. As a result the playing may have been a little less seat of the pants than normal, but that's ok too. After all, this IS a lesson book right?

I don't think there is one single answer that works in all cases. If there was, there would only be one method (maybe only one guitar... perhaps only one song).

This is meant to be a "learn by doing" experience. The lessons are contained in the music itself. Each chorus (complete 12 bar blues cycle) exploits a slightly different idea. This idea is described at the beginning of the chorus. If you like the way a certain chorus sounds, you can follow the idea while using your own licks and musical vocabulary. If you don't like it, chances are, practicing the idea won't get you usable results.

There are two points I would like you to think about:

⇨   Playing an effective turnaround in your solo is like musical punctuation. You are telling your listeners "I am finished with this chorus and I am about to begin a new idea." NOT including it can sometimes be interpreted as inexperience, or that the player is not paying attention to song form. Turnarounds do not have to be original. I tend to think of including it as "speaking with the right musical accent."

⇨   It is perfectly acceptable to use only the blues (or pentatonic) scale over the entire progression. It is also OK to use different scales over each chord. I think it's good to be able to inject as much or as little "scale spice" as is needed for the moment. Of course that is very much at the discretion of the player. If you can keep track of the form of the song and really know what chord is happening at any moment (without having to think about it), this process is much easier.

▶▶ **the solo: <u>first chorus</u>** / CD Track # 16 • *Backing tracks only CD Track 17*

1st Chorus: All G minor pentatonic

⏸ the solo: 2nd chorus / (~00:22)

⇥ the solo: 3rd chorus / (~00:41)

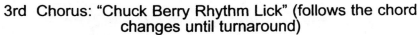

3rd Chorus: "Chuck Berry Rhythm Lick" (follows the chord changes until turnaround)

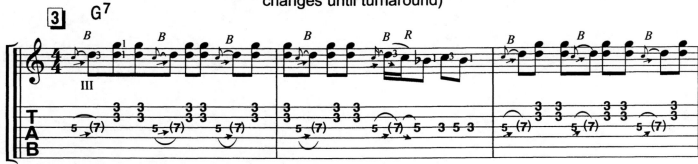

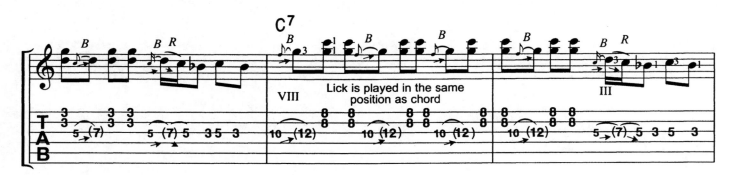

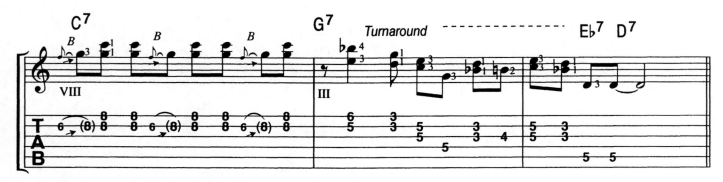

⇥ the solo: 4th chorus / (~01:00)

4th Chorus: Chromatics & bends; follows the chord changes

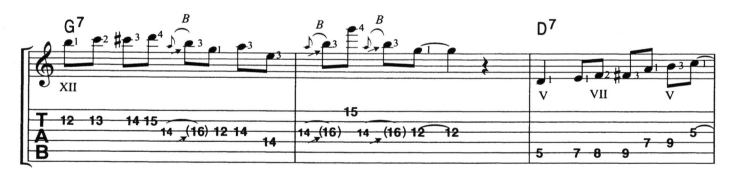

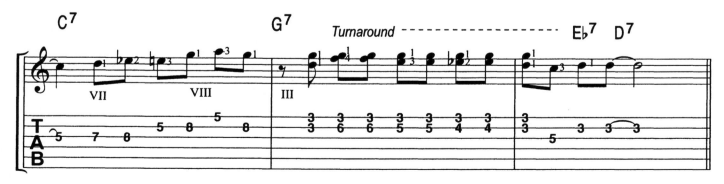

⇥ the solo: 5th chorus / (~01:19)

5th Chorus: Double stops & rhythm patterns

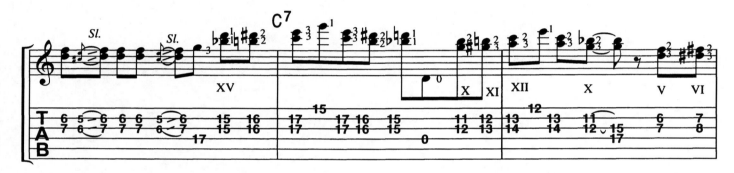

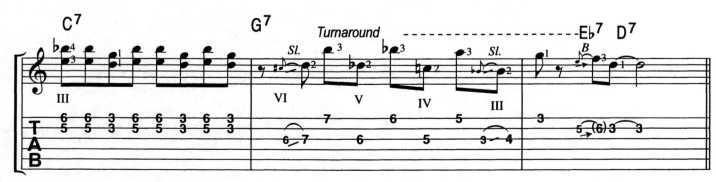

▸▸ the solo: 6th chorus / (~01:38)

6th Chorus: 16th notes, notes change in position
according to chord changes

▸▸ the solo: 7th chorus / (~01:57)

7th Chorus: Bends & melodic phrasing; follows chords

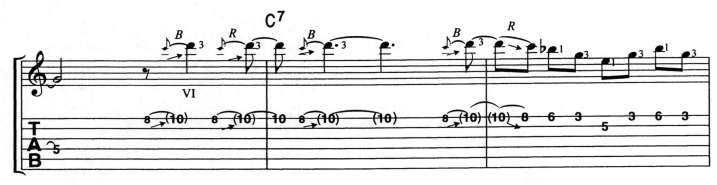

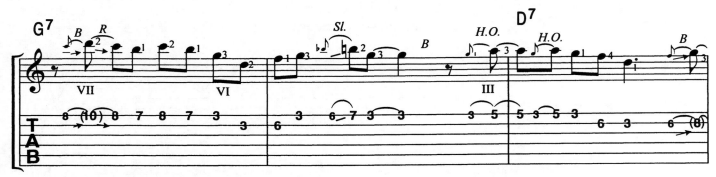

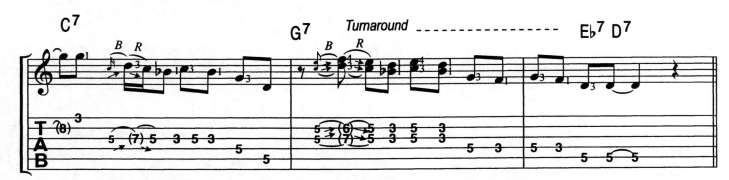

▸▸ the solo: 8th chorus / (~02:16)

8th Chorus: Alternate Pentatonics & bends (follows chord changes)

⏵⏵ the solo: 9th chorus (a) / (~02:34)

9th Chorus: Chromatics & 16th notes

the solo: 9th chorus (cont.)

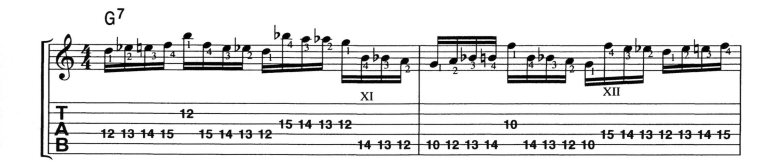

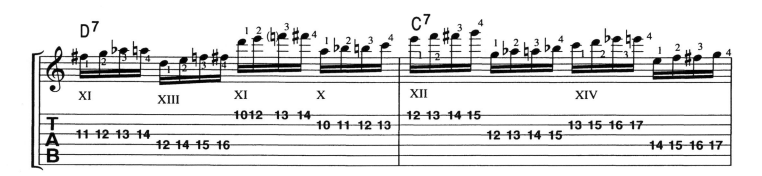

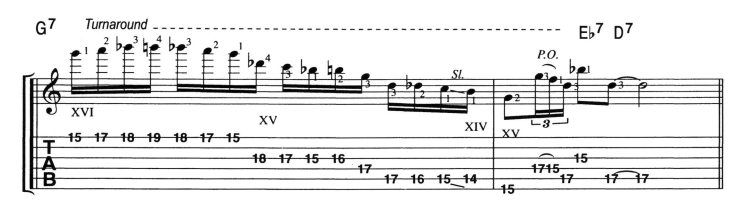

⇥ the solo: 10th chorus / (~02:53)

10th Chorus: High notes, vibrato & bends

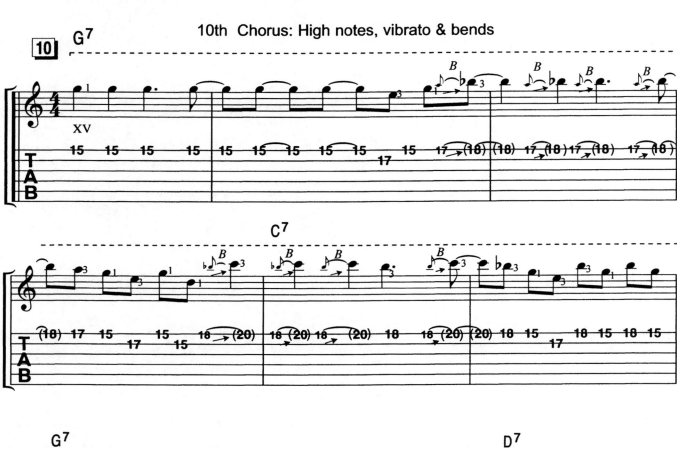

conclusion

In this book, we worked on these things:

⇨ The rhythm guitar parts, how they interact, and why it's important to know them.

⇨ The conceptual mechanics of the the Standard Blues Progression.

⇨ Turnaround licks, and why they're important.

⇨ A short series of of exercises that help build a specific set of soloing skills.

⇨ A transcribed Blues/Rock solo where each chorus exploits a slightly different idea.

One thing I have learned is that there really is no "right" way to solo. Whatever sounds good works. Just the same, creativity and inspiration without discipline or focus can often sound, well, unfocused. That is really the point of this book: To learn how to focus your solo so that the result sounds directed.

That is one of the most difficult balances to maintain; Having a clear focus and direction while being open to your creative "spur of the moment" muse.

One thing that is great about being a musician is that, unlike being a jet fighter pilot, we usually live through having a bad day. Knowing that helps give me the courage to fearlessly improvise. What that means is, "without the need to be fearful."

It's really OK. Just play and enjoy!

about the book

Blues/Rock Improvisation is a complete workout in that style from Jon Finn. You learn rhythm guitar parts, turnaround licks, soloing exercises and a fully transcribed solo from Jon. You learn not only what to play, but when, where, and why. This book is a big step forward in decoding the mysteries of what is a very simple but elusive style to truly master. For this project, a song was written, performed, recorded, transcribed then explained. By showing the entire song, then breaking it down to its elements you get a unique look at the creative process. Once you learn all the elements and understand why each choice was made, you will have a big advantage when continuing to develop your own style!

about the author

Jon Finn has taught in the guitar department at Berklee College of Music for many years. His band, "Jon Finn Group" gained worldwide acclaim from their concert tours and CD releases (Don't Look so Serious - Legato Records 1994 and Wicked - SEP Records 1998). In 1996, Jon began writing a monthly instructional column for the nationally published Guitar magazine. His band, his teaching and his published pieces have all been dedicated to the advancement of modern electric guitar. He's performed/recorded with renowned guitarists John Petrucci (Dream Theater), Vinnie Moore, Andy Timmons and Steve Morse (Dixie Dregs). Jon plays guitar with the Boston Pops Orchestra, performing in concert halls all over the world. His recording credits with them include two Grammy nominated recordings, "The Celtic Album" (1997 BMG Classics) and "The Latin Album" (1999 BMG Classics). He has also played in many contemporary national touring musical theater productions such as "Rent", "Mamma Mia!", "Aida", "Joseph and the Amazing Technicolor Dreamcoat", "Copacabana" and many others. Jon's other books, "Advanced Modern Rock Guitar Improvisation" and "One Guitar Many Styles" are also available from Mel Bay.

Visit jonfinn.com.